INDICTUS
NATALIE EILBERT

Book Cover Design: Alban Fischer
Book Interior Design: Sarah Gzemski

Published by Noemi Press, Inc. A Nonprofit Literary Organization.
www.noemipress.org.

INDICTUS
NATALIE EILBERT

To probe oneself is to recognize that one is incomplete.

— Clarice Lispector

If I could kill you I would then have to make another exactly like you.
Why.
To tell it to.

— Anne Carson

Table of Contents

To Read Poems Is to Follow Another Line to the Afterlife.
To Write Them Is to Wed Life with Afterlife.

Words are filthy.

With themselves.

With the past.

If I jump around in my details, it is because I have willfully refused details in writing.

I tell a friend I want to delete this whole book so that no one will see it

and he says I should hold onto that feeling.

Poetry allows me to enter into the afterlife. Line after line, I find specific names, construct a knowing from malignant odes—but no, I don't want to be found, personally.

Let me say of language that it is my currency and performs best when it is stripped of decorum.

The word STRIP is better as a noun than a verb, not simply in a literal sense but an etymological one as well.

Strip.

A long time ago, a boyfriend critiqued one of my violations, naming the event non-habitual.

I was seven.
I was thirteen.
I was fourteen.
I was twenty-one.
I was twenty-three.
Recently.

Details lock me into the violence of chronological events, but I refuse to let this be chronological.

Chronology, too, is filthy.

All these men, specifically so.

The cartoon of the crime: a man gauzed by hate moving inside the flattened surface of another's body, a shadow of a shadow.

Even in the highest form of truth, to access memory is to blunder its event.

10

INDICT, in its earliest use, exclusively meant to bring lawful charges against—but something marginalized groups know a lot about inserted itself. The language shifted to accommodate the reality of the court. Not an action with punitive consequence, but a means to write, compose, or dictate a poem. It was left to the imagination of the survivor to alternate the course of events. At this same point, poetry meant a fable or tale in verse.

INDICTUS points to the unsaid.
In this way, *to indict* is to write the unsaid.
These are the men I imagine gone now.
I envision a world where the men are gone who pulled language out of my mouth to push themselves in.
Men who said what I could not speak.
I push language back into the body I could never save—and I pull from the hole a roster.

I take these specific men who saw no mind, who lacquered my body with the possessive, giving me only the failure of narrative, sentencing my life to verb—I take these men and I form them into the wound of a line.

I allow myself the fantasy of the gone men, aware of what they've done.

I fantasize what my own forgiveness might look like if I loosened their gaze.

I reset the great books of our origins and vanish us all into the possibility of parable.

I live in the gap of the verb of my life as I always have.

And out of the blank of the gap of the verb of my life, I again present my men.

Man Hole

I left him unfinished. I just wanted to.
The snow outside fills the sewers
and, like my drive for power, will stop abruptly.
Starting now, I will drop picture frames
down the hole. Drop food processors and Le Creuset pans
and my chaste little letters. My interest
in godless practices undoes the ritual.

I have a hole where I store my typographies.

When he is beautiful, he adapts to a you-state,
*thou*s his way into my pants to mortify my skins.
He draws me over in charcoal, my dull sternum
pinks with creation. I have a hole capable of erasure.
His jaw hangs like a mantis there, there.

I make him just once pierced with hundreds of holes.
I make him to scrub and prick and lube his skin 'til he bends in his beautiful stalk.

Then I make him to crave my every protein as I fill him with clay and stone and ink.

Here is a mirror to wander through, a hallway to crack over his knee.

I make him to touch my strong arms as I spread him open with my knee.
I give him bloomers. I give him diamonds. I give him my desiccated brainstem
and ask if he'd like to go home now. He digs a hole in the ground and climbs in
and this makes him mine forever.

He needs to follow one smart line to the holes. The holes slosh his guts into foam.

I was lonely before I learned the care of men—then I craved loneliness.

A lover leaned me back on a bed and unrolled my pants. I wanted him except in fucking in the dark I straddle a serpent, pushed forward still by the crying monster slick with lather. This after my own great event when a man peeled me open in the dark. The word *lover* feels like glue in my throat to utter. The lover takes my clit in his hand like a shitty little bird and asks, *Where is your goddamn agency?*

The holes in my body swallow up traffic cones. They chuckle in their own membranous way.

One definition of a hole is:

> When men accidentally kill endangered wildlife,
> they fill the beasts with holes, sew in rocks, sink them into larger holes.

One definition of a hole:

> I used to use Maxi Pads against my hole, and I could smell
> the perfumed rot when a man slipped in through my window.

Another:

> I don't hear them in the vents. I don't hear them over me in the dark, emptying. I
> starve my body still, in case it drives them back.

My poor man, so full of addendum,
when you are mine, you become animate—
only capable of burning selfies in the shit lake.
                                        I say when.
And when I close the sepulcher it is done and
you are the agnostic whimpering he.
I place a hole over you, under you, fill it with rock.
Can't wait to return to my dumb bitch couch
where he is in the empty border I sit inside.

                                    The dog presents her dead.
                                        An amnesiac claims
                                  she was touched by a man
                              and the touch felt like power.

The beauty of holes is that I cannot enter one without ceasing to
exist in the seen world. A body can disappear and become
subsumed by a space, so the body is nothing but an act
of spectral negation. My cunt is a star, its darkness pressed to the floor
to temporarily light me, to lighten.

So the channels of men close. The lines of the men close.
I have a spit sample of my history and I hock and
I hock and I hock in the holes of my men.

To call a woman a hole is to suggest immediate use.
To call a man a hole suggests grave incivility—

incivilities I place like a knife at the windowsill.

When I weep, my calcium brittles. My men limn in sinkholes

until I reach myself in, place me a globe from a lord's
stunned bosom against their throats. As I lift their chins this way,
they say, *This is my freedom, my liberty—my delicate sovereignty.*

I store them in the hole outside my body, a decent hole.
It keeps them veal-dark. Vials and vials worth of DNA
clink and shudder. All these engorged wads of dead ocean.

When he is homely, he is a leader of men and glimmers a brawny integument of HE.
He is drawn from the rocks. He rapes a hole in me to fill me with rocks.
My consent is my sinking to the seafloor.
I hum to the bottom.

When he is homely, a hole forms in his throat for him to speak.
Stones fall out with his crude syntax.

I make him hundreds of times, drilling behind his temples to make future exterminations
simple. I make his cock hundreds of times. I freeze it mid-revision.

I make him hundreds of times, let his holes grow dusty from lack of speech.

I make him hundreds of times and he sits on a rock all bashful and glitz.

I make him hundreds of times until he is pretty and worth his weight in flesh.

And in his flesh I see him, that delicate sovereignty of his limbs.
And when I see him, I scoop out his throat. I take it in the hole and his eyes tell me
he's grateful. I *thou* him so hard I feel his fingers wrapping their worth round my neck.

My love is a hole I can only make once. I make it hundreds and hundreds of times.

● ● ● ● ● ● ● ● ● ● ● ● ● ● ●

First, I touch the cheek of my new hole.
I turn its lips to my mouth, roll my tongue in the dry black, gently the dry black.
I fold my hole over a bed, three fingers in, I express its naked beauty as it lurches.

Forward, always.
My face travels down to my hole and I clear away the skins.
I lick the hole above the hole. I, demonstrative; I, leverage.
I roll off my jeans and push myself in.
When I'm close, stars wrap around cow hearts.
To love a hole is to investigate the limpid, star-like abstraction of feeling.
To love a hole is to investigate the investigation of everything else.

The cows collapse in moony pasture.

There is no bed. There is no tongue.

(nothing)

We ignore vacancy when its convenience leads to pleasure.
An empty expression. In existing in this life, I've survived nothing.

22

My patience has become glandular. My inner resources spilt in twine. Split in twain.
The old feminist anthology splayed out with my 22-year-old-self notes.
I thought and I thought and I thought, but could never property
express my shelves. I gendered myself until little holes trepanned outward.
I'm a bad denim vest. I'm a bad feminine land. I art my way
out of my pants and my importance is mistaken.

Endless newsfeed of creation, I experiment with the long-durational
Photoshop of my body by feeding/mptying, emptying/eeding.
I place a hole on the ground to walk from the hole. The whole hole
is a mathematical impossibility and I ruin from the kinship. The split shin. The sin.

When I love a man, what I really love is myself when I can't fuck a man.
Desire volunteers its negation—and it is sweet, to hurt my body,
to bend it this way, that way. After all, the best stretch
moves your limbs as far from your center as possible, reaching feats
of opposition I am too sorry to hold. I dream I am more than my memories,
my menories. I whisk grace until it thickens into not-grace.
Just how sorry am I? Breathe here for twenty breaths.

Empty, I huff. Empty, I silence my body against the floor. Empty, I thin
myself to wisp myself out of the machine. Empty I apparatus
under the dead light. Empty I forget. Empty I Find & Replace. Empty I
a grown man's cock against my stomach. Empty I forget. Empty the ground
shakes a calculated doom. Empty I tectonic. Empty I sorry my way
to new bones in soil. Empty I read accounts of what happened. Empty I
what really happened. Empty I forget. Empty I despite empty despite.
Empty I oof. Empty I ugh. Empty I alien influence. Empty I replace.
Empty I hold my knees. Empty I come. Empty I water the tardigrades. Empty I
grow bigger.

Friends, I have memories now. Memories dehydrate living:
film is interstitial and brief, so we may choose to grieve.

Memories playact our agencies in any given
scene, and so, naturally, are dangerous.

My fingers dedicate motions to preserve my memories,
though it is no use. What was done to me slips away

like a second language learned but unspoken. I imagine my breasts
serrated off my body. The secret gunk below—that is who I must be. Please

swarm my chatty vulva. Its cranial notes move up my throat
like the clarinet I dreamed of once that became a complex.

Wasn't it the clarinet in the corner I finally understood when he lifted me up—
the reed snapping me into a rhythm made of too many hands?

Didn't I initiate the song? What happened to me is a dumb knowledge quest,
the slay runs wet. The language in the trees chants, *A quest with many holes.* I dip

my legs in man holes to annihilate the routine dance. Empty, I converge.
Friends, I have now. I dip into the man holes to replenish fading limbs.

One definition of country:

Dig a hole and replace. Dig a hole and replace. Dig a hole and replace. Dig a hole and replace.
Dig a hole and replace. Dig a hole and replace. Dig a hole and replace. Dig a hole and replace.
Dig a hole and replace. Dig a hole and replace. Dig a hole and replace. Dig a hole and replace.
Dig a hole and replace. Dig a hole and replace. Dig a hole and replace. Dig a hole and replace.
Dig a hole and replace. Dig a hole and replace. Dig a hole and replace. Dig a hole and replace.
Dig a hole and replace. Dig a hole and replace. Dig a hole and replace. Dig a hole and replace.
Dig a hole and replace. Dig a hole and replace. Dig a hole and replace. Dig a hole and replace.
Dig a hole and replace. Dig a hole and replace. Dig a hole and replace. Dig a hole and replace.
Dig a hole and replace. Dig a hole and replace. Dig a hole and replace. Dig a hole and replace.
Dig a hole and replace. Dig a hole and replace. Dig a hole and replace. Dig a hole and replace.
Dig a hole and replace. Dig a hole and replace. Dig a hole and replace. Dig a hole and replace.
Dig a hole and replace. Dig a hole and replace. Dig a hole and replace. Dig a hole and replace.
Dig a hole and replace. Dig a hole and replace. Dig a hole and replace. Dig a hole and replace.
Dig a hole and replace. Dig a hole and replace. Dig a hole and replace. Dig a hole and replace.
Dig a hole and replace. Dig a hole and replace. Dig a hole and replace. Dig a hole and replace.
Dig a hole and replace. Dig a hole and replace. Dig a hole and replace. Dig a hole and replace.
Dig a hole and replace. Dig a hole and replace. Dig a hole and replace. Dig a hole and replace.
Dig a hole and replace. Dig a hole and replace. Dig a hole and replace. Dig a hole and replace.
Dig a hole and replace. Dig a hole and replace. Dig a hole and replace. Dig a hole and replace.
Dig a hole and replace. Dig a hole and replace. Dig a hole and replace. Dig a hole and replace.

Dig a hole to dig a hole.

I didn't mean to assemble my whole career on lies, so now I blast holes
in the men. I blast holes in the pits of the men. I blast holes in the holes
who are the men. I move them in a process called autonomous fetishization,
and they enjoy the hazards of my queenly thinking. I grip their cheeks

and make them fish-mouth kind words toward me. So much of what I've done
has involved what I've not done, which is so deliciously Victorian I could faint. I hold
the heads of my men to my cheek

like fox-stoles and demand no answers, only the rubbing
of tongue against artificial tongue. Artificial losing isn't hard to master.
I am a bright red wet mouth that lies to everyone,
except the holes that keep me liminal.
The Zero plunged between my thighs.

• • • • • • • • • • • • • • • •

Katie L hooked her finger inside her cheek
      to describe what it felt like to sleep each night
      sick from every germ, sick again from the spread.

We were best friends, our mouths linking our hurt
      in the rows of teeth we bit with to bite through.

The body draws some funny weapons. Someone
      took her in a van, taped her weapon shut, left her
      on the grass one block away hours later. They
      called her fine, because that's how we monetize
      damage—a transaction of skin against survived skin.

They dropped a coin in her palm, its warm nickel
      bridled her with purpose so she never spoke again.

Was the van a white van? they urged as she stared.

Her stare was a white van or it was not. The Ls abandoned
      the house and never returned. No address. No answer
      to the white vans chewing through wilderness.

Sylvan weeds trembled through the Ls' dirt, grew toward
    clouded residence. A vacuum filled their acreage. A void ate their home.

Everyone called what happened *a damn shame. A damn shame*
        absorbs into the body, tumesces loudly, and
        no one speaks of girls' bodies as anything but accident.

A damn shame is when they describe Katie L as adorable
        and blonde. Jaundice halos above her bedpost night after
        night. I read her Simone Weil: *A hurtful act is the trans-*
        ference to others of the degradation which we bear
        in ourselves. The van doors slam, the men disappear.

I am learning what forgiveness means by means
        of looping thread through the bobbed heads of stickmen—
        no, I am learning what forgiveness means by
        pressing my ear to their limbs to hear the debt
of their pulse, to hum the slick red of such apology.

I take beauty into a landscape and split it open,
        the scent it makes to chew its flora—an act of transference.

The white van extends its limbs to taunt in the game of life and limb.

True emptiness doesn't exist on the planet—isn't that something? Holes
  are essayistic then, a drill's devotion—where we toss our prodigious girls.

Katie L was a hole that entered the white van. The men choked
  on her gases until little holes blinked through their skin.

They feared her vacuum. They emptied themselves of the vacuum
  by placing her in the gentle grass. They never even touched her.

Routines of devotion are lonely like this, as when my own smell
  calls back a man who blamed me for the odor of his bed.

Do I remember when he brought my face to his sheets and demanded
  I smell what I made? I do not and I loved it. I pushed a disc over memory
  so I could breathe freely over it.

What are we to do when our avatars form imaginary lines
  over streets and meadows to lure us back to a place?

What do we even mean when we call a thing a meadow?
  A meadow plucks petals from a flower.
Dead girl. Not a dead girl. Dead girl. Not dead. Dead.

Film offers a continuation—a way of reframing reframes of a scene
       that in order to happen must first happen. Film can rupture
       country, to remember what came before and after kingdom.

My country is a white van. All the presidents spill from the opening door
       when they see us walking. My hips sway back and forth,
       and I wake up to the terrible electricity of being seen.

When I cup my palms, I peer inside the hole they make. Temporary.

Harmless. I push a fist through bread to demonstrate my force. See how I

       knuckle my way into the first phase of power? Power is a hole
suitably buried. A father's flabby throat. I dream inside this relapse
       into film.

A hole is made of every ugly dead girl.

       Emptiness grafts itself to believers, the loneliness
of form and swallowed Eros. I don't know Katie L anymore,
       her name a rope in my gut I can't pull.

My dad texts me and asks me to name all the men in my book of men.
I drop my phone into the Sound in reply. I approach all questions with access

to a nearby hole. *Do you get it?* I ask inside Katie L's mouth.
I compose letters of forgiveness only after a drill sounds.

• • • • • • • • • • • • • • •

When you tell me
my life is a sob story
I grow wet around the rim,

I auto bio graph myself
against my skin.
I give my I a new look. I rosy cheeks.

Did you know I can critique
your paratactic engagement with life
and still make off as a beauty queen?

This is the source of my powerlessness.
Acidic mucus
drips in threads at the back of my throat.

My life is a sob story.
It continues on a thread.

My life is a sob story.

It continues.

I tug out the thread.

I cling to the fabrics. I rip down all the curtains.

Such is my hypotaxis, I spit into my palm

and massage the edge of myself around myself.

Let's face this sofa story together.
Memory is a dislodged pelvis
from a line of anesthetized bodies.
It moves out of sync with the living until
a genital blooms in the bone summit.
Move it one way, another.

White flares flick my temple as I wait
for annunciation, limbs boiling

station to station. Intelligence—
what I mean when I see the pulse
of a poem and it feels like a man I have to win over.
I do. When I win him over, I do not win.
He tests me. Queer lust blooms on my tongue. Forget.

Memory beheld a glimmering data. It
let grief conjoin and it began, a kind of home
in its continuum. I can no longer be the woman
who tells you what solidarity means.
It's a rock folded over a breathing hole.
And I need no air, only similitude.

Nothing happened. The alcohol shone
over the night. I cried once. A woman approached me
and said as much. A seam ripped.
Many seams ripped. A hole leaked
from my hole, spilling decadent oils.

My mind is quick to spoil. I am like the rock thrown
in my uncle's grave. I land without ceremony or miracle
with the other dirts. My diets. My flesh thins
around perception's hegemonic mutations.
I bury data inside me, birth information.

A rock beneath my feet glows new rhetoric—
I am golem I am clay I am
the breath of my own shitty god.

To believe what was done to me is curable,
assumes a shape. This assumes
what was done to me is truly done.

Clarice Lispector wrote:
I don't want something already made but something
still torturously made.

Jimmy me into a keyhole.
I want to be the name men call to scatter their ashes
I want to be the name
they can't close their eyes against.
How are they taking it? The flesh I made them into, the flesh
I tear from them to tear myself into myself.
A grammar of skins: I love them/it hurts me.

But this world is not conclusion. I pull my history through a valve
and give it edges, give it holes.
I love men when they let me see myself.
A dog learning discipline laps up such pretty pearls.

My hole is a gentle hole—
everyone here in my hole is a home into which I toss aesthetics.

This eats this better than this, says Bernadette,
and I am alone in the grass, patting the pubic
spring. Theme of midland crisis: in flight,
I am wayward from the engine that
propelled me to forgive. To enter anything
without the shock of ridicule, without the demand
to lie down. I lie down in black ectoplasm.
I gunk up the holes with alien scabs. A swell
opens into bungled relief. My effort transforms
into the representation of EFFORT. In this way, though,
I am the sand that fills the hole, and not even sand.

Biology is a discourse. We understand others by breaking them apart,
an evolutionary development. A seed blooms from the rupture of seed,
see it? See *dehiscence*: I must focus on the explanation of shapes
to alienate time to the one event. I grew up disappearing
into a body. Then several. I want to tell you what happened to me.

I grew up disappearing into a body. Then several. I want to tell you what happened to me.

But what should I say?

After months of inactivity, I spring from bed arrested by the cinema of your arm around my throat. I cannot help write down this borrowed violence. Isn't that the goal?

Formula 1: Something needed to happen, and then it did.
Formula 2: Something needed language to have happened.
Formula 3: Language is always re-examining a truth in mutiny.
Formula 4: If language is required to give what happened narrative context, then the past is not the past at all but always present, in the way glass is liquid. We do as glass does, pretend solidity by breaking down over time. How can we know any better?

If I am happy, I need only to stare long enough
at the word INESCAPABLE.

To escape still carries the infinitive cage.
Its origins, to get out
of one's cage, suggests the word
is its own small box. *To inescape*, then, is the shape beyond such effort.
To know with certainty that a center keeps us.

For the men to return I must construct a sympathetic brain.
I must remove any traces of Old English from the nodes,
eradicate *blód* and *grisl.* I must give them the loneliness of hands.

I want you to memorize a pathway. A woman scrambles
from the sea to a surface as two monsters duke it out, seemingly for her honor.

She is beautiful with fear. She has two options:
get fucked or die horribly. It is up to the viewer to decide
whether she is a plot-driving agent or a void in the momentum.

I have learned so much of myself from what I haven't said.

My body bends to a system because there are systems in place everywhere else.

Richard Feynman said the simplest answer to any question
that starts with why: *the sun is shining.*

Why [ ]?
The sun is shining.
I'm having trouble sourcing this.

When I bend at the hip I push out the property
of others in myself. I rinse myself of the necessary dirt
collected in my valves.
Sometimes the reality of the poem
is its resistance to consumerism; a poem is therefore unrealistic.

A poem is a hole in how it is dug up,
the soil purged, the soiled purge—movement likened
to a net uncatching. So it can't help be decorum.

A net without evidence of a kill is part of its setting.
This is when it is most dangerous. Language is the same
once it learns the best way to draw blood is to transform over time.

The weapon can't help enact decorum—and then a line moves over my mouth.

An examination means question but also suggests torture. When I examine the memories that broke me, I torture my question.

My grandmother sits in her soiled purge without memory. The long-term is a fuse line into and away from the body. When it ends, it can't end—only curl around the very vessels lengthening it. Despite my best efforts, my only definition for death is when the world quits giving the brain a combustible thread.

The sun is shining. My friend disembowels a cow in Montana. A house is made of so many things. If it is beautiful, I can't say. I disembowel the sink. The terror of drains is the terror of throats because it is modeled after the very thing that takes anything we swallow.

All week I have had dreams in which men are awkward soldiers who need my touch. I want very much to give them touch, to pronounce them a love I don't know if I possess. *Trauma*, Anne Boyer writes, *is like a mind which has a shadow and then is the shadow and then isn't a mind or its shadow but isn't at all.* In dreams I reach my hand out, as in the James Tate poem "Very Late But Not Too Late": *And when / she reached out and held my hand, I felt as though / my life had begun.*

I call this my postlapsarian insistence—to devote oneself to a world one must give oneself over to another world. Devotion is feminine. Devotion is obliteration. For this reason, I discovered the hands of men and nurtured them like alien rocks instead of returning. In science fiction, I had to travel to the top of a mountain to derive sap from a sleeping woman. The sap was key in reanimation, as was pain from an Arctic fox's tongue, as was thistle from the throat of a snow leopard. The poem exists still somewhere.

I called the sun *a blunt sun.* I just needed my life to begin.

My favorite word, second
to DEVOTION, is STONE. What we are
is either memory or invention. In Latin,
to *incubate* is to watch jealously.
It is a third word I admire for its utility
and it stays in my head, imitating itself.
Even if men have been removed, there is still
the foundation of men. Stone devotion.
My obsession with words is a kind of envy,
that they affect meaning as their former usage
is erased, retooled. I turned to him
in my childhood bedroom, a stone
now part of the root of memory. Distant
beep of microwave, a devotion to feed.
The foundation of man cooks before me,
it broods until little fingers tap
the skin. I ask that its luminance form
a head, so I can push back its lips and suck.
He I call man, I do as Bishop—I
watch it closely, genre my way to paradise,
the wick, the burn, the diction carried up.

I incubate cellular masses, my disciplined body.

But what am I to do about the blade that doesn't cut—

the blade that is a geometry only, diagraming threat?

I am like a hole with seams neatly built in

Last night I realized the phone never rings in my poems

A wheel turns and I am back in 1994, a child chewing granite

Examine formlessness as a wilderness in which something eats better than something else

Something else something else something else

This is disaster profiteering: to write FEEL so often, to enumerate the I, to kick the mattress off the frame. I don't write about fucking because it's too confusing—I write about the arrangement of fucking, the orchestral readying, being inside the push and suck, how consent is a means towards and away from contamination, how it brought me to the page. It is extremely infantile. I would like to never feel soft.

●　●　●　●　●　●　●　●　●　●　●　●　●　●

Perhaps it should be now I choose to continue the science fiction.

Dumb little smart girl

begins her adventure holding her crotch with both hands. Ow ow ow.

Milk pooling in her breasts. It is a moment of inescapable power. It is a moment made inescapable.

Dumb little smart girl

walks with both hands against her thighs. Others cover their asses with books.

Women hurt themselves to turn their wars inward.

The men fall away. They prophesied
    skin into capital, a topographical map, dead alkaline.

Dumb little smart girl fucks herself against a broken tree. She comes from her limbs, the third-eye bends metal into a beautiful phallus.

In the grass she sees a wrist curling out of the ground—a seedling. Dehiscence.

It is like a snake or the tongue of a dehydrated god and she wants badly to suck its joints back
    to wet flesh.

She recalls her heroic refusal of so many men and she recalls their heroic victory.

She attended one Take Back the Night meeting. No, she walked past one Take Back the Night meeting—then she chose an alternate route.

One definition of *victory*: to see refusal as a place to conquer. This is the place she must conquer by refusing place at all.

So she digs. She annunciates the dirt. *There.*

The men cramped and doubled over. She knew they handled death
the way they could handle holding her face down, the way they called
her cheekburn *stupid*. She rubbed feces off her nose. All fine.

Time is a meditation on how we choose to not remember, right? So
        it figures that we only lose shape in an attempt to say anything—to say nothing.

The girl who knows this also knows that she could be pinned beautifully.
She could wipe the grease of wrongdoings along the window and sneer
at the ordinary mess of such a gesture. She could draw the word PROFIT
in her palm print, she could squeeze her hips to applaud the scene.

Montaigne writes, *Where their profit is, let them have their pleasure too.*
And so the men arrive like falling bricks. Women enter bearing conference badges.

Confusion is a way to deny complicity. To literally be inside the fusion of things.

Not inside—without.

She would like to be done with assembly.

She finds the hand of a man so bearable she would throw her life
off a cliff clutching the hand to her.

This she calls *the surge*. She has forgotten much.

There is a heart for each good man buried prettily in silk,
a dark lozenge warming to black elixirs. Give me your hand.

She presses through colonial gardens, the site of paternal provenance.

She sips a gel so potent the shade membranes tingle her brow. She is queen.
She has always been queen.

Give it to me.

How hard is it to construct a narrative toward forgiveness

when ruin when rupture when appetite when third position

when smoke when no when oil when dog lips

when cracked lens when the hallway when he couldn't stop

himself when wouldn't when dress when fetish when not

when vacuum when electric fire when lines when memoir

when mildew when extremely when crashed sedan when you

when you when he when he when prosecution when small

when hijack when cigarette burn when threat when place

when there was a moment and another moment and a

moment followed soon after? These are cheap devices.

There is an awareness in the slick. I dream she dreams.

I dream she dreams her life hurt more. All those years ago,

when she was I, the acts were textbook, not cinematic.

They could be clearly defined—though their memories,

her memories' actors, did not win her any Oscars.

They simply were. She did not run or push them off.

The air moves with apoplectic trouble, it runs as clear as ever.

How hard it is to construct a narrative toward forgiveness!

We must look at the word DEFINITIVE. The words we grip around it.

Why would I do this, imagine the upper crust lightened
half a species, the men in sick droves crumbling as in that famous
photograph of buffalo from a cliff edge? And you could see no doom
riddling their bovine faces, the fact of their faces a mask for their faces.

At what point in this messy fantasy will I ever feel better?
I spoon elixirs through my lips, convinced of their elements.

...

Well.

...

When I was a girl, I was surrounded by horses. I mean they were on every side of my parents'
land. Corrals full of braying, the uric sweat warping the doors of my home. I knew to be terrified.
These were large animals, peripheral muscles shivering their form thicker. I didn't speak much. I
crushed on my brother's older friends. I trailed them and they, in turn, relented to my creep. I
followed them into the woods, toward the equine heat. They let me. They lost me. I
let them. I was a miserable kid.

What do I want to tell you?

The time they threw me around and took turns punching my guts wasn't traumatic—it was expected.

I don't write because there's a problem that needs to be solved. I write because I can't even tell you the problem. It is like the mathematical axiom of nothing—that to solve anything on the basis of nothing, we must first solve nothing. And there is nothing to be solved. And so, we attempt to solve it. It isn't that my problems are nonexistent. They have been stuffed into a rich and satisfying elsewhere, pneumatic and secure, their aspects only revealed over time. A smell like dryer sheets—the smell of the dying.

I cry in a nail salon because the woman is so gentle with my hands. I grew up in a house. There were horses on every side of the land. I uncovered my vagina for a boy. We looked deeply into it, equally disturbed that I was its carrier. I had a father. I had a mother. I had two brothers. One had terrible friends but they were each one so cute, except for one. Except for one who walked with an insidious gait and who was older than the rest. Except for one who, after the rest play-attacked me, kept going with the door closed. I had an aboveground pool. I had cats. I had plumbing.

I recently dreamed that an older figure wrapped my naked body in plastic and pressed himself against me so I felt his soft genitals. It was an act of mercy. This after—in the dream—I told him what happened in that room, what continued to happen in other rooms. I tried to wriggle my body away from his to no avail. I knew he wanted forgiveness. That I needed also to be forgiven. We are not supposed to talk about these dreams.

Years and years went by like this. My childhood was decent.

Years and years went by like this. My childhood was decent.

And yet.

My visions cannot be undone, so I think it must be that in order to fully function again I have to reverse myself. But I grow older. Memory is not static. It is like a box of smoke carried in sweaty arms across a river that, to flow, must flood. And so I flood. I envision the men who carry me away.

The Men Fall Away

The Rapist Joins AA

Received an email, formally written.
Was sorry for that night all those years ago. Signed *sincerely.*

Deleted the email. Went to my Trash. Deleted it there too.
Looked to my History. Deleted my History.

Focused back on those kitchen lights. Beaming grease. On the man.

Was the only night I ever drove drunk. The dark was not God's back turned away.

Drove slowly, imagined my car reeling home on a thick yellow string.
The machine I now carry also imagined this thick yellow string.

Parked delicately in a diner parking lot. Was worried an idle car
on a shoulder might spark interest. Was a very smart girl.

Walked to the back of the diner. Practiced a quiet retch to alert no one
of any trouble.

Let the poisons spill out of me with grace.
When no new liquids came, knew I was empty. Black hollows there

like a wet dead possum in snow.

Deleted the liquid. Deleted the snow.

Did not wait a moment longer before pulling myself back to the car.

Must have been I was a very dumb girl. There was an exit could have tried harder
to find. Friends all in the next room. Could have screamed.

When he pulled away had said *sorry* quite sincerely. Left him crying there, my name in his
mouth.

My curse to him was that I did not speak.

Silence is a hole that sucked hard to take him. Sucked so hard
his skin ripped from the bones in his face. Sucked so hard
all his great big dogs died of cancer. Sucked so hard
they pulled the overdose out of his stomach, stuffed

charcoal down his throat instead until he couldn't stop himself
from shitting on the doctor's table.

Sucked so hard his love for a woman became the charcoal inside him that forced him to uncontrollably purge in public

until his love for a woman became hate for a woman.

Sucked so hard he never even had a father. His mother a cat sick with worms
they had to put down.

Sucked so hard his back gave out, his herniated disks a little Greek choir.

That pain will only ever occur to him.

That the dumb little smart girl will find him there for years after watching him crawl.

Never spoke to anyone about this letter, the amends that must have been hiding

between his naked unwieldy body and the open kitchen door.

When the road was a line letting me follow it home.

Of course it rained.

Turned the familiar left onto my street. Parked the car in that night.
The dark was not where a deer concludes.

The dark did not instruct
on how to remove the bruises from my dumb little smart girl breasts.

Deleted the breasts. Deleted the night.

And so arrived home safely.

Genesis

God said LET so of course a pathway opened not for me—said,
God! Look on these rich men who stand at the tailgate, bursting

immunity. But I have said NO is a political nod and I have said
YES is part of the work of omission. I have not told you

why for years I placed a stone over my throat but
when I said *yes,* it was to obliterate certainty and when

I said *no,* it was to obliterate certainty. Years ago, my thighs opened
and the stone trickled out. I made a cake for the annihilation

split in sour earth. What I loved about autobiography was how
it didn't spill over, not really—rather the inculcation of passing through

formed a weapon against the conceit of weapons. I read your memoir
until I had your life by the balls—the moony tang of confessional.

I trolled the banks until a single hair could be pulled from my cunt
and I bent far enough over to show off my afterlife, to give the people

what they begged for. This is my goddamn landscape. I wrote about
my passage into envy on onionskins and boasted its nature,

a rust puddle I drank with certainty. If I exaggerate, it is so
you believe me this time, so my body finally forms into its fable:

meat fills the edges of narrative, and you can leer at my edges. It's
what I've always wanted. The spit and the lunch and glitch of your gaze.

Consent is a hole I've dropped all silverware through. I eat with arms
tied. I began this by pronouncing God into the silk of a wound

when I fondled commandment into an act of mercy. It was no big deal—
it was already there. I simply found a messiah and polluted the air

with my kind. I gave you a thimble with my nails inside and I told you,
Shake the contents. That desiccated mouth is mine, it says *yes* it says *no.*

It drips a sore into your palm, and another. Close your hand around it.
I'm writing a novel about paradise.

I have green branches between my legs. Sometimes,
a leaf falls through. I have a beard where
theory used to live, to explain why I wept all
the way through *The Left Hand of Darkness*.
My skinniness reveals the ontological use
of postindustrial emptiness through the lens of
capitalism and outbreak, so I couldn't possibly
touch a crumb—or misspell the motives of my brethren.
The last time my childhood friend and I got together
we discussed our rapes over pancakes. Naturally,
pancakes are all I can ever stomach now. As a girl
I was petrified of Le Guin's description of rain
as a flaw: *A flaw of rain.* Father gave me a gold coin
and told me to bite down. The perfect Jewess,
I interchanged gelt and guilt most beautifully.
I couldn't smile enough the day the final breath
exited the final man, but that's another story.
The men tried to save themselves. Their lives
a cold radiator, it made no difference. Chocolate. Gold.

But never mind that, here's the other other story:
a man led a girl into a closet and bit down.
Her cat escaped his leg when he left. It isn't
much of a story. It never became a story at all.

Neighborhood

I was a boy until they found me
        lost in the woods. Then I was just
            a stupid girl lost in the woods.
        The neighborhood kids were
just that, until one stripped me
        down, one found my sex tapes,
            one made me mouth the word
        VICTIM until the cable came back.
Narrative saturation, what I mean
        when I repeat the scene, a theater
backlit so each action is a shadow. A limb
            that grabs for the hypothetical map
until I am elected, animate, gaining selfhood.
        With his toe, my brother pushed
away my drinking bowl until
        I was a boy thirsting for its very tin.
The talk show host retires

as I set my damage to sound

all over the shitty velvet curtains, the apartment lined in rungs.

It is what the boys feared—my contrapuntal link.

When we are finished, a leather

takes hold, and I am not long

for the slutty skirts of this world.

In front of a black globe, I place a hat

on my head, turn

this way, that—I, oblong ghost,

return it to a hook with care.

Testament with Water under the Bridge

They get to name the sons and I get a short cry before falling
into line. I loosed my thighs by the river and scrubbed the

oil-slick fauna with my pubis as a cure. My fever
is I'm starving. I've gone slack in the arms, spooned mud to

begging lips, and beat my tongue into absolution. I walked
the rape-trenches and came back many times to redeem the witch

and my powerlessness clenched power to redeem her. My cervix
buckled under the gait of its thick visions and I could do nothing

but serve my kind more mud, more absolution. This is my chorus
of refusal: to know I am rent and crave the chasm that it makes.

Yes I exited the scene in a powerful gown, but when the sun
sets we fail each other. It is religious, my desire to find a better bridge,

to be misguided by the promise of suspension. To meditate,
I recall my soft inner cheek as it was pressed into my teeth by a silver hand.

I don't know if I can be allowed a permanent ordinance—the earth drains
the color from me as I give my Lord a better O Face. My sex is

a golden lampstand. I grip teeth around its poles, bleeding inventory
until a journey winnows through. I anoint the jealous when I stand

at the helm of invention, and I renew every snare to perform it
again. My ejaculations leave me empty-handed in this way

that daughters play the harlot with their gods. Karina dreams
she must perform in a white van for assailants, construct a tabernacle

against the wood of dominance, smile for the cameras to seduce her limbs
into pillars and rings and curtains. Of course. When the congregation

eyes me, I wiggle my hips until my calves announce my purpose. No wonder
I slurp when they bring the spoon to my lips. I gave up priestly garments

to be closer to the burning filigree. I singed my polyester tunic when
uncertain with what to do with my community. Last night a man

handed me his letter of apology. I'm an opportunist for gifts, so I put
the whole congregation in my mouth and lo, my power is I have not once bitten down.

Indictus

I read yesterday that crimes are committed at higher frequency during hotter temperature spikes. What was the language of my first crime? First, it was the house where I was born. I never dreamed. I never remember dreaming. This is not where it begins. Whenever I said I was up to nothing, my mother knew the opposite was true. She didn't know what that opposite might mean. I smeared four sticks of butter all over my bedroom wall in secret and she knocked on my door. *What are you doing / Nothing.* For years I found yellow knobs on my wall and then the house was gone by way of fire. We watched the inferno from the neighbor's driveway. This was years after that same neighbor removed my language—or it was only a year? Who is counting all the little footsteps toward error? When I sweat I am a half-species begging my body to stay alive, just a little bit longer.

Judges

I have a message from God for you. A minute
from now I will drown in a glass of daughter.

I gave up judgment to be closer to the floorboards.
I saw that I am not outside-outside. Noise of a club

circles back in like a saccharine plague.
The sound of man like the fat that hugs the

plunged sword. Oh, but how I entertain eternity—
a clear message nourishes as broth does, so I stir

and pluck out hot bones barehanded. I saw how
I whisper my laws, when my hunger strikes

a decade and half too late. When I pull the half-life
out of syntax, decay rises out of time, my scarab throat.

I saw at the park I let you lift me like rucksack.
The court spilled out of me even as I held it.

I was thick dough when you ran us away. I never
knew you. Under a branch in my sportiest dress,

my breasts flattened to quarry—a surface clean,
fit for every turning wheel. You handed me a vial

and I'm supposed to get it. I saw the persuasion crushed
through a whole body as I reminisce the entire.

How I've gnawed the rims of cups. My desire to forget
left me a cast-iron mouth. In this book, a message

from God is a very bad thing, the capitalizing hilt
against the temple, a segment so soft and body

I believe briefly that God has a message—why else would
the skull shape around a kill switch? In this book, take me

to eat, open a skin of milk and give me drink. When I ask
men in the pews to stand and fix their laps, faith is a spotted

garment, a material to boast certain rupture.
The blank wind sails innuendos elsewhere, a blade

made dull by prescription. The men blare techno forever.
On that day, I shook a prince until his whiskers

flew into the punchbowl. I quaked my flesh and smeared
like a white donkey left for the buzzing dark. I wrote

like I was waiting. Face to face with memory, the letter
misses. I saw I was ready to make use of loss.

In Truth I Wish Him Harm

How often was she told as a girl that cats were good swimmers?

Who can blame her disbelief?

And so it came as something of a shock to watch a tabby emerge from the East River, glistening.

The joke became that each time a woman can't articulate the truth of her calamities, another man dies.

The next joke became whether they will take turns cutting out the other's tongue.

The third joke is the old joke of women's great silence.

They have always been such fine swimmers, seals piercing the Arctic, the stalked animal's quiet grace of acceptance.

Cat got your tongue.

Man tumbles down a cliff with the storied heft of buffalo.

Gray bubbles surface from the disease of falling down.

This is not the story one wishes to tell.

One wants to beg for mercy now, but one can't.

In a world without men there is no need for mercy.

Such great numbers disappear one hardly believes in death anymore.

The joke is that women won the war on women.

When she is a girl, a man rolls up her shirt after crushing her to the floor with
his body.

Then the man lifts her from the tiles and throws her on the urine-soaked mattress.

Somewhere another man collapses to his knees, seizes, and he falls back as his pants
darken.

Then the man removes her pants and tells her to watch the television.

It radiates a blue light.

Blue. Blue. Blue. Blue. Blue. Blue. Blue. Blue. Blue. Blue. Blue. Blue. Blue. Blue. Blue.
Blue. Blue. Blue. Blue. Blue. Blue. Blue. Blue. Blue. Blue. Blue. Blue. Blue. Blue. Blue.
Blue. Blue. Blue. Blue. Blue. Blue. Blue. Blue. Blue. Blue. Blue. Blue. Blue. Blue. Blue.
Blue. Blue. Blue. Blue. Blue. Blue. Blue. Blue. Blue. Blue. Blue. Blue. Blue. Blue. Blue.
Blue. Blue. Blue. Blue. Blue. Blue. Blue. Blue. Blue. Blue. Blue. Blue. Blue. Blue. Blue.
Blue. Blue. Blue. Blue. Blue. Blue. Blue. Blue. Blue. Blue. Blue. Blue. Blue. Blue. Blue.
Blue. Blue. Blue. Blue. Blue. Blue. Blue. Blue. Blue. Blue. Blue. Blue. Blue. Blue. Blue.
Blue. Blue. Blue. Blue. Blue. Blue. Blue. Blue. Blue. Blue. Blue. Blue. Blue. Blue. Blue.
Blue. Blue. Blue. Blue. Blue. Blue. Blue. Blue. Blue. Blue. Blue. Blue. Blue. Blue. Blue.
Blue. Blue. Blue. Blue. Blue. Blue. Blue. Blue. Blue. Blue. Blue. Blue. Blue. Blue. Blue.
Blue. Blue. Blue. Blue. Blue. Blue. Blue. Blue. Blue. Blue. Blue. Blue. Blue. Blue. Blue.
Blue. Blue. Blue. Blue. Blue. Blue. Blue. Blue. Blue. Blue. Blue. Blue. Blue. Blue. Blue.
Blue. Blue. Blue. Blue. Blue. Blue. Blue. Blue. Blue. Blue. Blue. Blue. Blue. Blue. Blue.
Blue. Blue. Blue. Blue. Blue. Blue. Blue. Blue. Blue. Blue. Blue. Blue. Blue. Blue. Blue.
Blue. Blue. Blue. Blue. Blue. Blue. Blue. Blue. Blue. Blue. Blue. Blue. Blue. Blue. Blue.
Blue. Blue. Blue. Blue. Blue. Blue. Blue. Blue. Blue. Blue. Blue. Blue. Blue. Blue. Blue.
Blue. Blue. Blue. Blue. Blue. Blue. Blue. Blue. Blue. Blue. Blue. Blue. Blue. Blue. Blue.
Blue. Blue. Blue. Blue. Blue. Blue. Blue. Blue. Blue. Blue. Blue. Blue. Blue. Blue. Blue.
Blue. Blue. Blue. Blue. Blue. Blue. Blue. Blue. Blue. Blue. Blue. Blue. Blue. Blue. Blue.
Blue. Blue. Blue. Blue. Blue. Blue. Blue. Blue. Blue. Blue. Blue. Blue. Blue. Blue. Blue.
Blue. Blue. Blue. Blue. Blue. Blue. Blue. Blue. Blue. Blue. Blue. Blue. Blue. Blue. Blue.

Blue.

Another man requests Bach as he bleeds out.

There are routines and then there are rituals.

The beauty of infection is its unending will for change, its appetite regulates the world
   to hunger.

The next day at school, the girl paints an easel so thick with blue, the paper tears
   under the weight of its material.

It is not the same blue but darker made darker.

But blue is only belief frozen into the shock of change, and so it makes no difference.

The girl develops a paralyzing fear of dark blue storm clouds.

She misses her bus.

The paint doesn't dry for a week.

Years later she will write with the deep worry it was only the color she saw.

No man.

No men.

How long does this go on?

Forever.

Not forever, she replies.

Testament Thrown atop an Altar

All our good intentions blemish under doubt, so I start anew.
Boil down the memory of being tossed over a shoulder—render

the body so it becomes an act so the body becomes the altar.
They captured an orca and named it Lolita, its naming

an act of faith in order to erase its status as captive. It is a story
the way the animal strung upside down is worthwhile, to cut a

loving seam to wash the organs of our chosen goat. The sudsing
gut oils. I read *Lolita* in a park in a strawberry dress, stuck

on his description of Lolita's matted brow. I touched my own. The fabrics
of my face glowed green, my lips fattened, my dress bunched up in the warmth

of my grass. I forgive myself for the tenderness where I was forced
to trap my animal. Captivity is a way for seduction to form a skin,

so we can say the same of consent—a word that to utter suggests
its alternate sentence. I tongue the airbrushed idols and invite

the joggers onto my grasses. The truth is there was never a beginning,
the living always moved in the swelter of dominance. But what of

the animal law where you lift my chin and find my black eyes in search
of your spilling? This is a love poem, after all—your knee pressed

to my lumbar, my teeth bright in the cloth. You have the power to feel inescapable
and I arch at your knowledge. I lap up dark essential nectars and close

my fist around the hole between. How well you exaggerate me. A clay pot
touched by man must be broken, and I bend over, unclean, to offer prosperity.

World's Tiniest Violin

There are so many rooms in my house, muffler
and tread and exhaust pipe in one pile, meniscus
and tendon and scat in another. My mind ticks
with possibility, how to screw one part
into another without damage.

I was taken from my bed to a car once,
the man driving dark and fast to keep me.

The car parked in an empty lot. You never see
your own scared eyes,
never see how close your braces are to foreskin,
the promise of home made good.

But then he took me to his home so far from mine—
old enough to live by himself, old enough
to keep his toothbrush in the shower stall,
old enough to have me there in my pajamas,
with my small wrists that are still so small.

I love the orchestra of plates pushed away,
the quiet understood refusal, the knot of its *no*
deep in the withered thorax. I chew a bolt
as I strengthen the man's meniscus.
I am incredible. You should come over
to look on my works. My dad meanwhile

called the hospitals, the police, the morgues
in his search for me. I was only gone one night.
I watched porn, not in tears.
I kept my bra on, my socks. Considered
the hymen dull in his bed. With hunger
I remove a tree from the earth just to see it there,
groomed, and twain, and nothing.

Ezekielle

In my thirtieth year I plunged the scroll inside me and honeyed
its material with golden import. I've flattened under the weight

of my feckless comrades, yanked the rods of my torture into communion,
forked hair into my studious mouth, and spread apart my country to show you

my survival. Because of your detestable idols, I am a certified daughter
of man. I dry hump the mounds of my nations until I can taste the charcoal

of my rations. The sun has baked the bones of men and Lord how can I repay
you for sparing my kind except I will not spare you. I am that desolate waste

you bat your lashes against, I am the sword by which you've checked your lips
for smudges, I am the vinegar of your latest cleanse, the vile images of technology

announcing the detox siege. Wouldn't you know it, my gold flickers
with a level of decadence that only a cock can spoil—and a cock does spoil me.

I go limp in its arms, I hold myself upright and unclean as the bones of men
bake outside. You've never seen what hunger does to eagerness, the excellence

scraping refusal into empire. In a cloud of cigarettes, I told you we're already
in a dystopia. Did you see the sexy way I kissed the chain, did you see

my northern entrance and how I dug a hole in the wall to eat my forgiveness,
the hard twang of your weapon hot on my throat? That day I flared with inner court,

I was all portico in the gloaming, I wiped my brow with oilcloth and vowed
not to look on the many baking bones of men with pity or anger. There is something

so bronze about my outlook these days, the way I bunch up the linen to fuck
its embroidered corners. *What else can I defile?* I ask, as I wipe my chin against my elders.

I have done as you commanded. I've forsaken the men who made us to be
worshipped on altars, I've unclenched the word of my Lord and let their bantams

trickle down my leg, I've rented the brownstone to hoard unclean oxygen,
I've brushed those baking bones of men with schmaltz and issued a warning,

declaring us better. What I know of tenderness is what I know of violation,
the restless insect of touch and our end. That is what you're saying. I must

map a border so we can be the meat in it—but I've instead become editorial
director of prophecy, pulled out the Lord's curls and tied their tufts to the highest

fencepost. I've produced a popular reality show called *How Weak Is Your Moral Constitution?* and I've folded a net over my pursuers to force out apology each episode.

There will be no delay. The days go by and every vision comes to nothing. Down the street I am the favored daughter because my fulfillment requires

no power and no snares. I am the stuff of my idols, they cannot know what it meant to lean me over the chair and be so desolate they named the township after my shape.

To Become Myself, I Fear What I'll Become

Language only explains itself inside. That's what I've come here
to tell you. There is an incision.

In childhood, I strung a hose around my waist and tied the other end to the base
        of a tree.

There was a fallout shelter in the woods. I strung a hose around my waist.
To enter, my body a gesso against the concrete walls. So many wet leaves held me
brotherly below. I believe in the power of dramatic entrance.

Shale performs the offense of memory, the way feet
can shed a buried wall into the grief of touch. I'm lonely.
There. It was easy to say. I wrote many letters then to my mother

to confess these necessary disappearances. It has always been easy,
my desire to die. I waited in the earth with a crown of tiger lilies.

We formed from the mistake of form, the mind pink from the chemical spills
of each tree, or flicker. Before I could beg, I had knees. My skin grew over a pebble

and it slips in my grease like a dead math. I love my city.
It gives me a cool slap, names the kneecap pebble: There was a time
when land outside clasped inside and stayed just there, a part I could elect to keep.

You see, there are so many images to reconcile. They writhe to be seen
beneath the tarp my brothers sewed, blue into other blue, some cheap sky
ripped from the jaws of a comatose mother. And isn't memory gorgeous?

Skin over the knee over the fragment, a joint that can break both ways to fail us—
like the seams of a closet of dresses, it waits to tear.

I followed a hose to an underground pit and got in.
I wanted the hose to snap. Wanted the cool dark the way a deadbolt wants nothing.

Eden

I interact with the symbols of confession,
erupt from exhaustion. Human toil improves
the whiteness of my eyes. I deep-fry a tooth
in marrow oil, chew it to a paste, smear it over your hole.
I made you to be better, but you were the same from my spit.
You stalked the long grass, grinned in your violence.
You moved your stick limbs, fluttered your lips
into a rounder pronoun. You are relearning language
to become yourself again, raised by the smoke of my history.
You wanted this exercise turned compendium:
What male figure was worse, impacted my jowls, pushed
pyrite through to imbue my tongue with fresh metals?
I cough a gold pebble into my palm and stare at the shine.
I am amazed at your courage—all of you who have told me
my mistakes were the wrong mistakes. But I articulated perfectly
why failure is so important to me. There was a failure done
to me first, and so I grant failure the way light grants a prism.
What if I told you that I enjoyed it at the time?
I was seven. Or I was six. I was thirteen. I was fourteen.
I was twenty-three. Would you disabuse me? I told you my alibi:
a pool party, locked eyes, a shirt pulled overhead. I told you
it's acrylic blue on cheap paper and it never dries. It's important

that you call me a liar. I blink seeds to a shape. My every memory
is an offense to what happened. You leaned me
over a couch, gripping my cunt—isn't that right? You asked,
Is this what you want? And I wept, for I was finally found.

Liquid Waste:
A Postscript

Indictus

I erected an epic to annunciate terror with fantasy. I was reading Aldous Huxley when I erected an epic to annunciate terror with fantasy. I was reading Aldous Huxley when I erected an epic to annunciate terror with fantasy. I was reading Aldous Huxley when I erected an epic to annunciate terror with fantasy. I was reading Aldous Huxley when I erected an epic to annunciate terror with fantasy. I was reading Aldous Huxley when I erected an epic to annunciate terror with fantasy. I was reading Aldous Huxley when I erected an epic to annunciate terror with fantasy. I was reading Aldous Huxley when I erected an epic to annunciate terror with fantasy. I was reading Aldous Huxley when I erected an epic to annunciate terror with fantasy. I was reading Aldous Huxley when I erected an epic to annunciate terror with fantasy. I was reading Aldous Huxley when

Indictus

Forgiveness is its own curse, you see. I will forgive you all even when you deny what was done, what you did. To learn about permission I had to first drink language. I had to limp in the gullible place of entrance. To forgive, I poured milk in a saucer for a creature that never came. You will be forgiven only when you tip your head back and breathe the sour bowl left once for succor. Let its air nurture you now. That you might bow, that you might only ever desire its terrible metals. See? See how I forgive you?

Indictus

Huxley called Lenina *pneumatic*. Huxley called the sofa *pneumatic*. These two descriptions are fewer than ten pages apart. I left home before this meaning had any connection, before bruises had the shock of commandment. My little sofa story—in the bosom of whom did I scream?

What does pneumatic mean | The air ran thin in my lungs

What does pneumatic mean | He recommended I shower

What does pneumatic mean | The TV flashed *Girls Gone Wild*

What does pneumatic mean | Wore Velcro fasteners—the sound a snowy tape, loosening

What does pneumatic mean | Allowed these identifiers to define me

What does pneumatic mean | Yelped when I saw his face in my window

What does pneumatic mean | He made fun of my paranoia

What does pneumatic mean | It was spring when I wasn't found in a morgue

What does pneumatic mean | In the future, this could be a book

What does pneumatic mean | In a series of events, the composition spreads

Liquid Waste

Again I chew the cud before I waste beneath myself.
What was it like to look him in the eye? Ask. What was it like?
Memory enjoys the sacrum, running its fingers along
stretching tissues. At 6. At 13. At 13, 14. I bend at the hip,
plea for black eyes, animal eyes. In gym, my body
folds over, bones muscle through skin. A girl tosses
a penny toward me and calls out to *fetch*. My nickname
is Penny because I picked up coins once in my Jew-girl skin.
Because a boy forced his way into my mouth and pulled out
language. Animal language. Slut language. I walk the halls,
hysteria pushes out my body an ecstatic gel. How am I
supposed to auto bio graph the skins of dead identifiers?
Infusoria. Delirium of rot. In memory I lift the dead
arms of grief, I bite down on aluminum sheaths,
Mina Loy draws my worm portrait, her hairs fall toward me.
My body spills waste. Brown blood along crotch lines.
My body spills waste. Metabolized yellow. Poor animal

zodiacs. Indecent incidents cradle me to sleep, cold liquids
warm quick against my hundred cunts. My skin has a charted
geography to which I am always loyal. I honor how it goes on
without me, secretes metabolized sky from crown to tailbone.
Death demands we remember erasure, prebirth cloth out of which
we can't pull language. My body spills waste. I remember.
The way oceans receive oceans, my body spills.

Liquid Waste

Again I chew the cud before I waste beneath myself.
I sit at a café and pour out. An impartiality of organs twisted
into weird suns. A man I called mentor pushed me forward
on a couch and reached up. Whenever I fold over, I think
of his hands working his body up, my body working his body
up. I disgust the image. It spills. I understand it as
shame. I stared at a bed of marigolds as my mother told me
of my cousin's suicide. My feet inched the black soil,
the full faces in each flower. How cheap, to be arranged.
My body spills. They could never be wild and radiate shame.
Shame unto shame as oceans unto oceans. My cousin
strung up in a room. Marigolds extrude a fear-full nature.
I was alarmed by my lack of care. I was so
young in my dimension. I was still in death's
dimension. I bragged to my mother my nonexistence.
Death had yet to show me the shame of being alive.
The impact of my nonexistence carved my existence.

My body spills. There was an unspeakable, indistinguishable
knot in this phase. I came to see this as choice.
Choice stroked on a liminal plane. In answer, my animal eye
reached through oyster layers toward oil, slime-wet rock
of humanity. And so, human form pitied me as I humanly formed.
Marigolds blinked above my origin story. Whatever was I
but the texture of blanched skin?

Liquid Waste

A man stares at me as I lock my door.
His hand moves from his side to his crotch, he pantomimes
kingdom. All day I let sweat drip in little lines of menace.
In my head I make a tree in place of faith.
The amorphous lump of thought. See how I live in devotion
to scene? I exist without nouns—the float keeps me
grateful, the vacuum a larger commotion of sympathy. In the house,
I check the locks. Love is a midnight shadow in the crack of a door.
The plump hand smudges into a star above me, my pores spit out
the trickling sky. In bed, I pluck red dots from the dark.
The X of my body rubbed by a morning stag, a beautiful ruined
strand over strand. Now when I have no prompt, I stain the mattress
with concept. Something mildews. I was born with black eyes
open, meaning I peeled back and stared through vaginal light.
I was given a name, that slime-wet rock yawned new technology.
Did I earn new status when he shouldn't have [   ]? I did not.
My body spills cheap fuel. Something mildews. A stranger

follows me up the stairs of my building. I tell him to leave.
He tells me he'd like to come in. My door leaks a hundred suns.
L'esprit de l'escalier means *staircase wit*—a comeback conceived
after the event. I say the word *leave* on the staircase without wit,
panic yellow in my mouth, the staircase spirals to the infinite
as invectives bleed from my teeth. What is this phrase, then?
How do its words actualize event and discourse? I see the stairs
green behind closed eyes, his begging face, and the miracle
of his turning away to leave. Yes, I darken with excess thought.
I stroke the cheek of a wall.
What else can I be today but gratuitous
language in open air? How else can this end but with spilling?
Hundreds of dead moons spilled from my hundreds of cunts.
It's not that he shouldn't have. I chase these beasts into a spiral
to the infinite stairs, pull fur from my lips.

Liquid Waste

You want to be turned in the dust because
the dust makes you holy, the dust dries you
out, the dust dusts your dust as oceans unto
oceans as shame unto shame. The body is
holy—it spills because it is mine, reduced to clasped
appendage. The white lurch of a face is male. See
how he sees me as dust dusts the dust, the dust's instructions?
May he be holy. May he plunge headlong
into holes in search of language and may he
find language as when my mother finds language
stretched from her/my book of mouths.
May my mother read her/my tears as sins
and may sins be the sins of his lurching
white faces. I tear the sins from his mouth as sins
form from the wreck of the resolution of power.
My mother tears bread and shoves the bread
through his mouth and out his hole and so

may my mother be the metabolism the man needs
to grow older. And so may the oceans crowd with bad
fish. May the holes shape themselves into a body
to better spill. The man drips headlong in the bready hole
of my mother. Glutinous zodiacs. Animals leap
into flower form. I auto bio graph my cud, I chew.
I carry myself across the room in secret worship.

Black Tourmaline

Do not come back, my brother says.
Do not come back, my brother says.
Sunset makes me cold. I walk a bridge
toward it. To be lonely like the sound
of leaves, I walk over the leaves. The landmass
thickens as I forest myself. I hear a voice crackle
through my phone and I look for a moon,
a dusted rim. Depression glass on which
I learn the word SALVAGE in an earlier decade. *I have left*
so much of the world behind, one star whispers.
I await the inevitable figure. He steps over
limbs with a gift. Darkness like trapped
rainwater, I thus behold a threshold.
It is clear what I must do to receive him.
And the gift in his hand I must open
my mouth to take.

Notes & Acknowledgements

"For the men to return": In *Zombi 2*, Susan Barrett finds herself confronted with an underwater zombie and a shark. The scene flashes a violet aperture, bruised in its seeking. She is naked save for her scuba gear and white thong. The zombie is between her legs, wrestling her down as she pulls at seaweed[1], grasping for purchase. What I remember is the shark, its hunger of flesh comforting against the other hunger of flesh, though we are made as viewers to see this as the same hunger as we also see ourselves as men in possession of pleasure. What I remember is the animal calm when the shark bites down on its assailant's dead flesh, negotiating its survival, that it swims away seemingly unscathed. What I remember is I was sure the shark was male.

I owe the concept and phrasing of "Every memory is an offense to what happened" to Dolan Morgan, who is such a genius that a mind-blow like this comes out of his mouth with utter ease over a beer.

The second section of "Genesis" ("I have green branches between my legs...") is for G, my oldest friend.

"World's Tiniest Violin" is for every survivor of sexual assault who believes what was done to them was deserved. What happened to you is real. How you've chosen to store the memories of that violence are yours, and you are not wrong for how you feel or act as a result of violation.

---

[1]Seaweed or the clothes I wore that night. Pulling at what was already discarded, without purchase.

"To Become Myself I Fear What I'll Become" is for Marina Weiss, who gave me the courage to revisit an attempt at writing the suicidal child. That's a tall order. My bravery is your bravery.

"Man Hole": The second section is for Dolan Morgan.
"A hurtful act is the transference to others of the degradation which we bear in ourselves" is from Simone Weil's *Gravity and Grace*. I'm grateful to Nina Puro who, when I desperately needed a voice, sent me a smattering of Simone Weil quotes. Because of course she did. And of course it worked.
The line "the transcendence inside me is the living and soft 'it,'" is from Clarice Lispector's *Água Viva*. I will quote her until I'm dead.
The line "the limpid, star-like abstraction of feeling" is also from Lispector's *Água Viva*.
The section that begins, "When you tell me your life is a sob story..." is for Monica McClure.
I did eventually source the Richard Feynman concept, which is ironically from his book, *The Pleasure of Finding Things Out*: "All the things that we see that are moving are moving because the sun is shining."
The Anne Boyer quotation, "[Trauma] is like a mind which has a shadow and then is the shadow and then isn't a mind or its shadow but isn't at all," is from her excellent book, *Garments Against Women*.

"Judges" is for and after Theresa Hak Kyung Cha. The line "Face to face with memory, the letter misses" is a reference to *Dictee*, Cha whose language drilled strange iridescent holes into powers across time and space.

"Liquid Waste" was inspired by Aaron Apps's *Dear Herculine*, and I am indebted to him for giving me some of the chewier words in this series.

Grateful acknowledgments to the following magazines, who published versions of the poems in *Indictus* in their wonderful pages:

-Anti: "World's Tiniest Violin"
Better Magazine: "The Rapist Joins AA"
The Boston Review: "Genesis" (originally published as "Vagenesis")
Cosmonauts Avenue: "Liquid Waste" ("Again I chew the cud..."), from "Man Hole" (section beginning "Katie L hooked her finger...")
Denver Quarterly: "Liquid Waste" ("A man stares at me as I lock my door...")
Dusie: "In Truth I Wish Him Harm"
The Foundry: "Black Tourmaline"
Granta: "Judges"
HTMLGIANT: from "Man Hole" (section beginning "I left him unfinished....")
jubilat: "Liquid Waste" ("You want to be turned to dust...")
The Kenyon Review: Second section of "Genesis" (originally titled "'Edenic'")
The Lifted Brow: "Ezekielle"
The Los Angeles Review of Books Quarterly: "Eden" "Liquid Waste" ("Drip. Something mildews...")
Pinwheel: "Neighborhood" (originally published as "-hood")
Pool Poetry: "Testament with Water Under the Bridge" and "Testament Thrown atop an Altar" (originally published as "Hexodus" and "Leviticuss")
Verse: from "Man Hole" (the remaining sections of "Man Hole")
Washington Square Journal: "Liquid Waste" ("I sit in a cafe...")

Thank You

I write this in June 2017, six months into Trump-era politics where we have been shown once again that the country does not care about victims and survivors of sexual assault. As is the case every June, I remember (alongside my dear friend Morgan Parker) Anne Sexton's lines from her poem, "The Truth the Dead Know": "It is June. I am tired of being brave." Grief is an exhaustion that requires further annunciation, an attention to verb. It is. I am. It is extremely difficult to imagine a book called *Indictus*, which points to my history of trauma, as an object bound not by grief and terror, but by paper and glue. I know that if you are reading this, it means you are holding this book in your hands. I have held this book inside me since I walked toward home and away from a car seventeen years ago. There are people in my life who have helped me, perhaps more than they'll ever know. Some will read this book. Others are in different seas entirely.

Thank you to my friends, new and old. To Siena Oristaglio, our late-night talks about such angular pain were invaluable. To Amy Brinker, Marlo Starr, and Lily Lamboy, my heart and soul and funk. To Molly Rose Quinn, my strong talented brilliant friend. To Morgan Parker, my tirelessly brave June sister. To Jayson Smith, who keeps me alive with boundless support and beauty. To Sarah Fuchs, newest numinous-est friend, what a fortune to open your door. To my fellow UW-Madison fellows, Derrick Austin, Jamel Brinkley, Sarah Fuchs, Marcela Fuentes, and Barrett Swanson: I am lucky, and luckier for you. To Emily Raw, for the fabular feral friendship. To Tom Oristaglio, who came to my first ever public reading from this collection and has continuously encouraged me. To Allyson Paty, a most gentle and necessary sun. To Mike Lala, tremendous field of sunflowers. To Mark Cugini, who in publishing my chapbook *And I Shall Again Be Virtuous*, granted me the first relief of this burden. To Carrie Lorig, extraordinary umwelt. To Nina Puro, for holding me up. To Dantiel Moniz, Carrie Schuettpelz, Jennie Seidewand, Emily Shetler, Jack Ortiz, and Rodrigo Restrepo, so fortunate we met. To Brandon Taylor, a light and delight. To Ricky Maldonado, the cheek to my bekele. To Tommy Pico, I would go to jail for you too. To Marina Weiss, for tender vigilance. To Karina Vahitova, eternal postmodern teen of my heart.

Thank you, Dolan Morgan, for pulling me out of too many wretched holes but for also teaching me how beautiful a void can be together.

Thank you to my family. I would like for us to be able to one day talk about this book. But not yet. I love you all very much.

Thank you to the Wisconsin Institute of Creative Writing for giving me a space for the 2016–17 year to live and breathe and teach. I'm grateful to Amaud Johnson, Sean Bishop, Amy Quan Barry, Judy Claire Mitchell, Jesse Lee Kerchevel, Ron Kuka, Danielle Evans, and Ron Wallace, as well as to the Halls family for bestowing me with the generous Jay C and Ruth Halls Fellowship.

And since we're on bravery, thank you thank you thank you to everyone at Noemi Press, who made this book something I could be proud to hold: Carmen Giménez Smith, you are more brilliant than a diamond mine. Thank you for believing in this book, believing in me, believing me. Diana Arterian, you gave this book its soul and heart, and are the best editor I could have asked for. Sarah Gzemski, I can barely spell the word "subtle" and I know typesetting this long-limbed beast must not have been easy. Suzi Garcia, thank you for your promo wizardry. Alban Fischer, my favorite cover designer. Thank you to Daniel Borzutzky, Dorothea Lasky, and Morgan Parker for your generous and extraordinary blurbs. You made me feel briefly immortal.

Thank you.